WHAT IS PURIM?

WRITTEN BY
SHARI LAST

FESTIVAL OF FUN

Be honest, have you ever heard of Purim?

Don't worry if you haven't. Purim is one of the lesser-known Jewish festivals – but I think it is the most fun. That's because Purim is kind of like Halloween, a birthday party, going to the theatre, and a bunch of playdates all rolled into one!

On Purim, Jewish people are supposed to be happy! The day is celebrated with food, wine, gifts, feasts, and often a large dose of silliness.

ARE YOU READY TO LEARN ALL ABOUT PURIM?

THE PURIM STORY

Purim celebrates how the Jews of ancient Persia overturned the evil plot of Haman. Haman was a villain who tried to destroy the Jewish people simply because he didn't like them. Learn more about the Purim story over the next few pages!

WHEN IS PURIM?

Purim is on the 14th day of the Hebrew month of Adar. It lasts for just one day.

The Jewish calendar is lunar, so it doesn't always match up with the "regular" solar calendar. Purim usually takes place at some point in February or March.

DID YOU KNOW?
Some cities celebrate Purim on the 15th of Adar. Turn to the Purim Around the World page to find out why!

Jewish days begin at sundown the night before, so Purim starts at night, once the day of the 13th has ended, and continues over the following day.

PRONOUNCING PURIM

Are you saying it right?

It is not *pooh-rim* – sorry!

And it isn't *pyure-im* – nothing to do with purity!

It is more like *per-im*. The "u" should make the same sound as the "oo" in *good*.

Here's how it's written in Hebrew:

פורים

THE PURIM STORY

So why do we celebrate Purim with parties, treats, and fancy dress?

To answer that question, we have to go back to ancient Persia, around 2,500 years ago. King Ahasuerus ruled over a huge empire of 127 lands. His subjects included the Jewish people, whose holy Temple lay in ruins...

Ahasuerus's prime minister was a man named Haman. Haman hated the Jews. He particularly despised Mordechai, a Jewish leader who refused to bow down to him. So Haman began hatching a wicked plot.

Esther was a young Jewish woman who lived in the capital city, Shushan, with her uncle, Mordechai. King Ahasuerus was searching for a new queen and he called for all the young women in the land to present themselves at his palace.

Esther did not want to go, but she had no choice. Mordechai told her to hide the fact that she was Jewish, so she would remain safe. Esther tried her best not to stand out, but the king saw her and chose her to be his new queen: Queen Esther.

Meanwhile, the prime minister, Haman, was plotting an attack on the Jews. He wanted to wipe them out completely. To pick the date for the attack, he drew random lots. The date chosen was the 13th of Adar. Haman sent out a decree, sealed with King Ahasuerus's approval: On the 13th of Adar, the people of the kingdom must rise up and destroy every single Jew.

DID YOU KNOW?

The ruins of Shushan – where most of the story takes place – can be found in present-day Iran.

WHY IS IT CALLED PURIM?

Haman believed in random chance, which is why he drew lots to choose the date for the attack. Jewish people, on the other hand, believe God is in control. The word "Purim" means "lots" in Hebrew, and it highlights how Haman's reliance on chance and luck did not help him defeat the Jewish people, who had their God on their side.

Mordechai found out about Haman's plot. He told Esther about it and begged her to go to the king and try to help.

In those days, it was very dangerous for anyone – even the queen – to approach the king uninvited. The king could punish, or even execute, her. But Esther was brave. She agreed to risk her life to save her people.

Esther prayed to God for three days. She made herself look as beautiful as possible and then she headed for King Ahasuerus's throne room. She knocked on the door . . .

Esther approached Ahasuerus and to her relief, he welcomed her! She invited him and Haman to a party. The king was pleased, and Haman was flattered.

They both enjoyed the party, and then Esther invited them to another party.

At the second party, Queen Esther told the king there was someone who wished to kill her. Someone who wished to destroy her entire people.

"Who?" demanded the king, furious at such treachery.

Esther pointed at Haman and shouted, "Him! Haman wishes to destroy all of the Jews, including me – for I am Jewish!"

Ahasuerus, who loved Esther, was horrified. He sent out a new decree that the Jews should fight back when attacked – and he sentenced Haman to death.

On the 13th of Adar, the battle began, but the Jews were strong and filled with purpose. They fought back against their attackers and defeated them. The following day, the 14th of Adar, the Jewish people celebrated their victory and – more importantly – their survival.

UPSIDE-DOWN DAY

Purim celebrates how the Jews overturned Haman's evil plot. So on Purim, people do things that are "upside-down" – to symbolise how all of Haman's plans came down on his own head! You want to know how?

First of all, Jewish children (and many adults!) dress up in costumes. The costumes show that things are out of the ordinary, or upside down! I once saw someone dress up as an upside-down clown. It was pretty impressive!

Whether we're going to synagogue, school, or out and about, we wear our costumes all day on Purim.

There are no rules about the costumes. They can be cool, cute, funny, scary, silly – anything! It's so much fun to walk around on Purim and see everyone all dressed up.

FAMILY FUN
Some families choose to dress up all together and go for a "Purim theme". I once saw a family where the parents were police officers and their tiny baby was a cute little burglar!

WHAT DO WE DO ON PURIM?

Jewish people enjoy having fun on Purim, and there are four activites they try to do over the course of the day: Giving charity, giving mishloach manot (gifts of food), hearing the megillah, and eating a feast!

DID YOU KNOW?
On Purim, children often team up to perform a skit or a song to raise money for a charity of their choice.

1. CHARITY

Of course, we should always think about people who are not as fortunate as us. On Purim, our most joyful day, there is an extra command to give generously to whoever asks.

2. MISHLOACH MANOT

This literally means sending presents. On Purim, we give a few of these presents to friends or family. A mishloach manot is a parcel containing at least two different kinds of food.

I like thinking up fun mishloach manot ideas. Once I gave my friends a mishloach manot containing cookies and milk. It was easy to make and they all loved it!

Some people make really big mishloach manot, while others do clever ones, or even tie it into their Purim theme! I once received a science-kit mishloach manot, full of sweets and treats that could all be used for cool experiments (for example, Mentos and a bottle of Coca Cola!) That was awesome – and messy. The family who gave it to me were all dressed up as famous scientists. (Some people really go all out!)

3. MEGILLAH

Megillah means story. Jewish people aim to listen to the Purim story twice on Purim. Once in the evening and once in the morning. The Purim story is the Book of Esther from the Hebrew bible, which is hand written on a special scroll of parchment.

GRAB A GREGGER!
A gregger is a traditional noisemaking device that many children bring to the megillah reading (some call it a grogger). The top bit spins round and makes a clicking noise.

I go to synagogue to hear the megillah with my family (in our costumes!) We listen as the megillah is read out in Hebrew. It takes about 45 minutes. Sounds boring, right?

But there's something fun too: every time the name "Haman" (the villain of the story) is read out, everyone shouts and boos! We even bring along noisemakers, whistles, and horns so we can be as noisy as possible.

> **MAKE YOUR OWN**
> Learn how to make your own noisemaker on the crafts page near the back of the book.

4. PURIM FEAST

On Purim afternoon, most families will head to a feast. It's common to invite friends and family and have a really big feast all together.

Some families do themed meals, decorating the tables – or even their houses – in amazing themes, such as outer space, a jungle, or a circus!

CAN YOU FIND THE FOLLOWING PURIM THEMES BELOW?

> **DID YOU KNOW?**
> Adults are encouraged to drink wine at the Purim feast because it is a day of celebration.

Often, during the meal, there will be a knock on the door. Groups of teenagers or adults will come inside and perform a small skit or song to raise money for charity – remember there's a special reminder on Purim to give charity? These performances are called spiels, and they help make the Purim feast very entertaining!

SUPERHERO   **JUNGLE**   **UNDER THE SEA**   **CIRCUS**   **LADYBIRD**

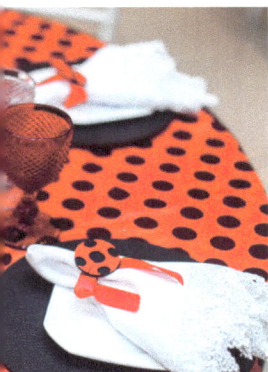

TRADITIONAL FOODS

On Purim, it's traditional to eat hamantashen. These are triangular-shaped biscuits or pastries that are filled with something sweet. Traditional fillings include jam, chocolate, or a sweet poppy-seed paste called mohn. Hamantashen can also be glazed or iced.

Lately, I've seen people being very creative with their hamantashen – from peanut butter and jam flavour to birthday cake toppings to exotic combinations like tahini and lime.

Personally, I prefer a doughy pastry to a crunchy biscuit-style hamantashen. And I'll take jam-filled with sprinkles any day.

BAKE YOUR OWN

There's a hamantashen recipe at the back of the book if you'd like to try them. What flavours will you choose?

HAMAN–WHAT–EN?

Hamantashen literally means Haman pockets (because they are pocket-shaped pastries).

On Purim, we celebrate the survival of the Jewish people. It's traditional to eat foods that symbolise Haman's downfall, and that's why we eat his "pockets" – it sort of makes fun of him!

In Hebrew, hamantashen are called *Aznei Haman* – which means Haman's ears. This symbolises Haman's downfall in a much more gruesome way!

PURIM AROUND THE WORLD

On Purim, Jewish people around the world celebrate the triumph over Haman. It is a joyful day with a serious message: We must stand up to the modern "Hamans" who use hate to undermine and destroy others.

Of course, different countries and cultures have their own Purim traditions. Let's find out about some of them!

JERUSALEM
Although Purim falls on the 14th of Adar, the date is different for those who live in walled cities. This is because the Jews who lived in walled cities battled and defeated their enemies a day later than those in unwalled cities. Jerusalem is a walled city, so many Jerusalemites travel to nearby cities on the 14th to enjoy Purim, before travelling back home and celebrating it a second time the next day. Sneaky!

FRANCE
Children write the name "Haman" on smooth stones. During the megillah reading, they strike the stones together whenever Haman's name is mentioned, aiming to erase his name by the end.

EASTERN EUROPE

Purim often falls during peak winter in Eastern Europe, so the children would build a Snow-Haman, as ugly and scary as they could! Part of the Purim celebrations included lighting a bonfire near the Snow-Haman and watching him melt.

USA

It's not often that "having fun" is top of the agenda. Many synagogues and Jewish organisations make the most of Purim and try to get as many people involved in the festivities. Think, big, extravagant Purim parties.

TUNISIA

Children used to build miniature Haman figures out of paper, straw, and rags. The meaner they looked, the better. In the evening, around a bonfire, they would chant: "Long live Mordechai and Esther! Cursed be Haman!"

ITALY

Time to throw some nuts! If you're ever in Italy over Purim, look out for adults riding on horseback, playing the role of Haman, while children throw nuts at them. Sounds fun.

IS IT PURIM?

If you live in a or near a Jewish community, you'll know when it's Purim! You'll see families walking around in fancy dress, hear music blaring in the streets, and you might see teenagers collecting money for charity.

PURIM GREETINGS

I hope you've enjoyed learning about Purim. If you have any Jewish friends and you want to wish them a happy Purim, here are a few ways to say it:

"HAPPY PURIM!"

"PURIM SAMEACH!"

Pronunciation: Per-im Sum-ay-uch
(This means "Happy Purim" in Hebrew)

Note: the "ch" in "Sameach" is a sound you make at the back of your throat. Or you can just use an "h" sound.

"AH FREILICHEN PURIM!"

Pronunciation: Ah Fray-lich-en Per-im
(This means "Happy Purim" in Yiddish)

Note: the "ch" in "Freilichen" is a guttural sound you make at the back of your throat. Or you can just use a "k" sound.

LET'S MAKE HAMANTASHEN!

Ingredients

- 3 eggs
- 1 cup sugar
- 2 teaspoon vanilla essence
- ¾ cup oil
- ⅓ cup water
- 1 tablespoon baking powder
- 5½ cups flour
- filling of your choice
- icing of your choice (optional)

Method

1. Beat eggs and sugar until creamy. Beat in the vanilla essence, oil, water, and baking powder.
2. Add flour one cup at a time until the mixture becomes a dough.
3. Cover and refrigerate for at least 1 hour.
4. Roll out the dough and use a circular cutter or a cup to cut out circles.
5. Put a teaspoon of your filling in the middle of each circle (don't overfill!)
6. Pinch the edges of the dough together to form a triangle shape around the filling, leaving some filling still visible.
7. Place on a baking sheet at bake at 175°C (350°F) for 15 minutes.
8. Ice, glaze, or sprinkle as desired!

PINCHY PINCH!

FLAVOUR INSPO!

Dulce de lece with coconut flakes

Victoria sponge (strawberry jam and cream)

Cinnamon bun

Maple pecan

Savoury

Chocolate orange

Ferrero Rocher

S'mores

WHAT CAN YOU THINK OF?!

PURIM CRAFT IDEAS

DECORATE YOUR OWN MASK

There are lots of printable masks available online. Choose a character or animal, and print out the mask. Cut out the eye holes carefully and then get colouring. Use stickers to decorate, or even glitter to add some sparkle! If you're feeling really crafty, you could always try to create a mask of your own face using papier mache! Good luck!

BUILD YOUR OWN GREGGER/NOISEMAKER

Anything that makes a noise can be used to drown out the name of Haman! Let's build a noisemaker using a plastic bottle. Pour lots of small, hard items inside and then seal tightly. Dry rice, beans, pasta, pebbles, or even pretty beads are perfect. Seal, decorate, and start shaking!

MAKE A DIY COSTUME

Think about the items you have lying around at home that might make a good costume. Old sheets? Cardboard boxes? Sometimes the simplest items make the best costumes. Get creative!

GET BAKING

Giving gifts of food is traditional on Purim, so what better way to celebrate than by baking Purim treats? You could make hamantashen or decorate biscuits with awesome Purim designs. You could even come up with some fun mishloach manot ideas.

First published in Great Britain in 2024
by TELL ME MORE Books

Text copyright ©2024 Shari Last
Design copyright ©2024 Shari Last

ISBN: 978-1-917200-01-1

Picture credits: Thanks to Adobe Stock, Adam Winger, Anton Gi, Austin Schmid, Conor Brown, Efren Barahona, Ewa Pinkonhead, Frank McKenna, Gemma Regalado, Hasan Almasi, Jeremiah Lawrence, John Benitez, Jordan Rowland, Karsten Winegeart, Krzysztof Hepner, Laura Siegal, RD Smith, Sigmund, SJ Objio, and Steven Libralon at Unsplash, and Amina Filkins, Daisy Anderson, Mikhail Nilov, Monstera, Skitterphoto, Vidal Balielo Jr at Pexels.

All rights reserved. Without limiting the rights under the copyright reserved above, no part of this publication may be reproduced, stored in, or introduced into a retrieval system, or transmitted, in any form, or by any means (electronic, mechanical, photocopying, recording or otherwise), without the prior written permission of the copyright owner.

WWW.TELLMEMOREBOOKS.COM

www.ingramcontent.com/pod-product-compliance
Lightning Source LLC
Chambersburg PA
CBHW050749110526
44591CB00002B/29